COMING OUT AND SEEKING SUPPORT

Other Books in the LIVING PROUD! Series

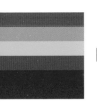

LIVING PROUD! GROWING UP LGBTQ

COMING OUT AND SEEKING SUPPORT

Robert Rodi and Laura Ross

Foreword by Kevin Jennings
Founder, GLSEN (the Gay, Lesbian & Straight
Education Network)

MASON CREST

Mason Crest
450 Parkway Drive, Suite D
Broomall, PA 19008
www.masoncrest.com

Printed in the United States of America

First printing
9 8 7 6 5 4 3 2 1

Series ISBN: 978-1-4222-3501-0
Hardcover ISBN: 978-1-4222-3503-4
ebook ISBN: 978-1-4222-8376-9

Cataloging-in-Publication Data is available on file at the Library of Congress.

Developed and Produced by Print Matters Productions, Inc. (www.printmattersinc.com)
Cover and Interior Design by Kris Tobiassen, Matchbook Digital

Picture credits: 10, JMAB/VMAB WENN Photos/Newscom; 13, Ben Schumin/Wikimedia Creative Commons; 16, Mixmike/iStock; 23, PR Photos; 26, Jason Moore/ZUMA Press/Newscom; 31, Wikimedia Creative Commons; 32, omgimages/iStock; 36, David Wimsett/ZUMA Press/ Newscom; 39, Bev Sykes/Wikimedia Creative Commons; 43, Andrey Bayda/Shutterstock; 45, Joe Mabel/Wikimedia Creative Commons; 48, FS2 WENN Photos/Newscom; 51, Allison Long/TNS/ Newscom
Front cover: ejwhite/iStock

COMING OUT AND
SEEKING SUPPORT

CONTENTS

KEY ICONS TO LOOK FOR

 Text-Dependent Questions: These questions send the reader back to the text for more careful attention to the evidence presented there.

 Words to Understand: These words with their easy-to-understand definitions will increase the reader's understanding of the text while building vocabulary skills.

 Series Glossary of Key Terms: This back-of-the-book glossary contains terminology used throughout this series. Words found here increase the reader's ability to read and comprehend higher-level books and articles in this field.

 Research Projects: Readers are pointed toward areas of further inquiry connected to each chapter. Suggestions are provided for projects that encourage deeper research and analysis.

 Sidebars: This boxed material within the main text allows readers to build knowledge, gain insights, explore possibilities, and broaden their perspectives by weaving together additional information to provide realistic and holistic perspectives.

FOREWORD

I loved libraries as a kid.

Every Saturday my mom and I would drive from the trailer where we lived on an unpaved road in the unincorporated town of Lewisville, North Carolina, and make the long drive to the "big city" of Winston-Salem to go to the downtown public library, where I would spend joyous hours perusing the books on the shelves. I'd end up lugging home as many books as my arms could carry and generally would devour them over the next seven days, all the while eagerly anticipating next week's trip. The library opened up all kinds of worlds to me—all kinds of worlds, except a gay one.

Oh, I found some "gay" books, even in the dark days of the 1970s. I'm not sure how I did, but I found my way to authors like Tennessee Williams, Yukio Mishima, and Gore Vidal. While these great artists created masterpieces of literature that affirmed that there were indeed other gay people in the universe, their portrayals of often-doomed gay men hardly made me feel hopeful about my future. It was better than nothing, but not much better. I felt so lonely and isolated I attempted to take my own life my junior year of high school.

In the 35 years since I graduated from high school in 1981, much has changed. Gay–straight alliances (an idea my students and I pioneered at Concord Academy in 1988) are now widespread in American schools. Out LGBT (lesbian, gay, bisexual, and transgender) celebrities and programs with LGBT themes are commonplace on the airwaves. Oregon has a proud bisexual governor, multiple members of Congress are out as lesbian, gay, or bisexual, and the White House was bathed in rainbow colors the day marriage equality became the law of the land in 2015. It gets better, indeed.

So why do we need the Living Proud! series?

- Because GLSEN (the Gay, Lesbian & Straight Education Network) reports that over two-thirds of LGBT students routinely hear anti-LGBT language at school

- Because GLSEN reports that over 60% of LGBT students do not feel safe at school
- Because the CDC (the Centers for Disease Control and Prevention, a U.S. government agency) reports that lesbian and gay students are four times more likely to attempt suicide than heterosexual students

In my current role as the executive director of the Arcus Foundation (the world's largest financial supporter of LGBT rights), I work in dozens of countries and see how far there still is to go. In over 70 countries same-sex relations are crimes under existing laws: in 8, they are a crime punishable by the death penalty. It's better, but it's not all better—especially in our libraries, where there remains a need for books that address LGBT issues that are appropriate for young people, books that will erase both the sense of isolation so many young LGBT people still feel as well as the ignorance so many non-LGBT young people have, ignorance that leads to the hate and violence that still plagues our community, both at home and abroad.

The Living Proud! series will change that and will save lives. By providing accurate, age-appropriate information to young people of all sexual orientations and gender identities, the Living Proud! series will help young people understand the complexities of the LGBT experience. Young LGBT people will see themselves in its pages, and that reflection will help them see a future full of hope and promise. I wish Living Proud! had been on the shelves of the Winston-Salem/Forsyth County Public Library back in the seventies. It would have changed my life. I'm confident that it will have as big an impact on its readers today as it would have had on me back then. And I commend it to readers of any age.

Kevin Jennings
Founder, GLSEN (the Gay, Lesbian & Straight Education Network)
Executive Director, Arcus Foundation

GLSEN®

GLSEN is the leading national education organization focused on ensuring safe and affirming schools for all students. GLSEN seeks to develop school climates where difference is valued for the positive contribution it makes to creating a more vibrant and diverse community.
www.glsen.org

Olympic medalist div
Daley came out publ
gay in 2013 in a vide
on YouTube. In the c
spoke about his sex
explained how when
love with a man, "so
just clicked. It felt ri

1

WHAT IT MEANS TO COME OUT

 WORDS TO UNDERSTAND

LGBT: An inclusive term used for lesbians, gays, bisexuals, and trans-gender people. (It is sometimes written LGBTQ, to include those who are *questioning* their sexual orientation or who identify as queer.)

Activists: People committed to social change through political and personal action.

Liberal: Open to new ideas; progressive; accepting and supportive of the ideas or lifestyle of others.

Alienation: A feeling of separation and distance from other people and from society.

October 11 can seem like just another day. It's not an officially recognized holiday. When it falls on a workday, banks and businesses are still open. On weekdays, school is still in session. There are no special sales in de-partment stores, and freeways aren't jammed with holiday travelers. But for thousands of people, October 11 is one of the most important days of the year. It's National Coming Out Day—set aside to encourage those people struggling to suppress their sexual identities to instead embrace them and share their true selves with their loved ones and the world.

"To anyone out there, especially young people, please know this," said football player Michael Sam at a recent National Coming Out Day celebration: "great things can happen when you have the courage to be yourself." These sentiments are echoed by an increasing number of high-profile gay people who have come out in the full glare of public attention, including Olympic diver Tom Daley, singer Sam Smith, actress Ellen Page, singer-songwriter Rufus Wainwright, actor Wentworth Miller, NBA player Jason Collins, actor Zachary Quinto, and many more.

The date for National Coming Out Day was selected in honor of the 1987 March on Washington for Lesbian and Gay Rights, which brought half a million demonstrators to the nation's capital. It was a pivotal moment in the movement for gay rights, and it led **activists** Rob Eichberg and Jean O'Leary to conceive of a national coming-out event that began the following year. In a few short years, annual celebrations were being held in all fifty states and a number of other countries around the world.

What Is "Coming Out"?

"Coming out" is defined by the Human Rights Campaign (HRC), an LGBT advocacy group, as "the process by which a person first acknowledges, accepts and appreciates his or her sexual orientation or gender identity and begins to share that with others." It is an incredibly important personal journey that means something different for each individual.

National Coming Out Day in Washington, D.C.

The HRC identifies three main stages to this complicated process. The first is *Opening Up to Yourself,* when individuals fully recognize and accept that they are gay, lesbian, bisexual, or transgender. As with each of the stages, this takes a different amount of time for each person. Some people may reach personal acceptance when they are still children, whereas others may not acknowledge their sexuality or gender identity until they are adults.

Once a person comes to terms with his or her own identity, a lot of careful consideration usually occurs before proceeding to the second stage, which is *Coming Out.* This involves actively discussing one's sexual orientation for the first time with significant others. For some individuals, this may happen in phases. For example, some people come out to friends early in their lives but wait years before telling their families. There is no right or wrong way to come out.

After working through the first two stages, people are finally able to begin *Living Openly*. Once their friends and families are aware of their identity, LGBT people then make the personal choice of how it will influence their lives. This is an ongoing part of the process and varies significantly depending on the individual. Some people continue to keep their personal lives private, accepting their LGBT identity as only one aspect of themselves. Others embrace their new identity in a much bigger way.

 CLOSE-UP: COMING OUT AS A PROCESS

We've described the three stages of the coming-out process, as identified by the Human Rights Campaign. The Wikihow website offers an even more detailed guide geared especially toward young people, called "How to Come Out as a Gay or Lesbian Teen." Its steps are as follows: (1) Make sure of your sexual orientation. (2) Make sure you will be safe if you tell people. (3) Before coming out, think of what questions they might ask, and have answers in mind just in case. (4) Start with close friends. (5) Come right out with your statement. (6) Allow time for people to process and assimilate this revelation. (7) Understand that this is something that will have a huge impact on certain aspects of your life. (8) Live *out* without being in people's faces about it. (9) Be able and willing to discuss your orientation with sincerely interested individuals. (10) Remember: Coming out is a process. It takes time—don't rush.

Feeling Proud—and Vulnerable

Adrienne Hudek is one of those who plunged headlong into her new gay life. "After I came out, it was all about rainbow pride," she says, referring to the gay-pride symbol of the rainbow flag."I participated in pride marches, volunteered for gay organizations, took part in protests, had rainbow bumper stickers on my car—everything. I couldn't wait to tell people I was gay, whether they needed to know or not!"

Adrienne was twenty-one, and the enthusiasm she felt is common among young LGBT people; coming out can feel like the celebration at the end of a long journey that included many roadblocks and struggles along the way. To provide assistance during the stages of the process, the HRC distributes a *Resource Guide to Coming Out*. The guide makes it clear that when coming out, it's normal to feel scared, vulnerable, brave, proud, confused, relieved, and uncertain—all at the same time.

"When I made the decision to come out, I felt about a hundred emotions all at once," says Adrienne. "It was so exciting, so scary, so invigorating. I knew my whole life was going to change."

Telling Friends

Compared to the coming-out process of many people, Adrienne's experience was not very difficult. The first person she told was her openly gay roommate, Brad. She knew he would understand, and yet she worried about the impact her announcement would have on him.

Adolescence is a difficult time for many individuals—a time when establishing one's own identity as separate from one's parents can be stressful and full of conflict. For LGBT teenagers, the challenges of adolescence can be even greater.

"It sounds weird to be afraid to come out to someone who's gay, but I really wondered if it would change things, because liking guys was something he thought we had in common!" she says. "But it was more than that. This was the first step. And I wanted to take fifteen more steps, but at the same time I was scared of what would come next. So I needed this to go well so that I would have the courage to keep going."

She thought about it for days, wrote drafts of what she would say, practiced in front of a mirror, and imagined the different reactions he might have. Finally, the day came.

"I was so nervous that it took me a few minutes to get it out. He was very patient, and he waited for me to say it. And then he just laughed," she says. "He gave me a hug and said, 'Yeah, I already knew that. It's pretty obvious.' And then he went back to working on his computer. It was no big deal. That made me feel much more confident about telling other people."

Like Adrienne, some people find that their friends are one step ahead of them when they finally come out. Others, unfortunately, do face rejection and lose friends during the coming-out process, and that can be painful; however, the pain is often lessened by the many new friends they meet when they embrace their new gay community.

Family Reactions

The love and acceptance of her friends helped Adrienne to get to the next step, which was telling her parents. Though her mother had always been open-minded and supportive about gay issues and causes, Adrienne didn't know if that would apply to their personal lives, too. She had friends whose parents seemed **liberal** and forward-thinking until confronted with the news that their own children were gay.

"I knew a guy whose parents were always talking about equal rights for everyone and loving your neighbor and being a good Christian," Adrienne says. "So he thought it would be no big deal to tell them he was gay. He was sure they would understand and even be happy that he told them. But when he did, they went crazy. They said he was just trying to get attention, and that it was only a phase. They told him that if he was going to be gay, he couldn't live in their house—so he had to leave home when he was sixteen. I couldn't have handled that."

Fortunately, she didn't have to. Just as Adrienne hoped, her mother simply listened, asked a few questions, and let Adrienne know she was loved. Then they talked about dating, just as they always had. Adrienne's only regret was not having accepted herself earlier so she could have come out even sooner.

"I look around now and see these kids who are eleven or twelve years old, and they are living completely out," she says. "People wonder how they can know at that age, but I knew. And I wonder what my life would have been like if I'd come out when I was that young. It's different for everyone, and you have to go at your own pace. But I really admire these kids, and their parents and friends who accept them, because they get to grow up knowing who they are."

Fear of Coming Out

Thanks to strong relationships with family and friends, young people like Adrienne have coming-out experiences that are very positive. But that is not always the case. In fact, many people never come out or delay making the decision because they fear what will happen as a result. People have thousands of reasons for not coming out, and one of the biggest is losing the acceptance of friends, family members, or churches.

"I couldn't imagine what my parents or family would say if they found out about these feelings," says Sarah Carlin, who came out while still in high school. "My dad always joked and called gay people 'queers.' My mom was no better."

Like many parents, Sarah's mom and dad made anti-gay remarks without giving it much thought. They never considered the possibility that Sarah might be a lesbian, so they were never concerned about the impact these statements could have on her when she was growing up. That mindset is not uncommon, but it can be changed through education and awareness. Organizations such as PFLAG (formerly known as Parents, Families and Friends of Lesbians and Gays) provide support and information from people who have been through this process with a loved one themselves.

 CLOSE-UP: COMING OUT AS A TEEN (OR YOUNGER)

LGBT youth are coming out younger than ever before. Recent studies have shown that the average age for gay and lesbian young people to begin the process of coming out is now 16; back in the 1980s, it was between 19 and 23. This means that many more young people are coming out before they finish high school, which can seriously affect their academic and home lives.

Another study found that half of students who experience homophobia and bullying have skipped school because of it. Schools that openly acknowledge and include LGBT students, and are outspoken about opposing bullying, create a positive environment in which all students feel safe and able to learn.

More than 4,000 U.S. high schools (and 120 middle schools!) have gay–straight alliances (GSAs). These student organizations provide gay and lesbian teens and their straight peers with a safe environment in which to meet. Every year during prom season, newspapers across the country carry stories of same-sex couples attending school dances, and community organizations hold gay proms for LGBT teens.

"This is the first generation of gay kids who have the great joy of being able to argue with their parents about dating, just like their straight peers do," says Ritch Savin-Williams, professor of developmental psychology at Cornell University.

Risks and Repercussions

As part of its Coming Out Project, the HRC recognizes additional risks. In some states, people can be fired from their jobs for being LGBT. LGBT people may be the victims of intolerance or **hate crimes** from peers and family members who don't understand or approve. Young people have even been thrown out of their homes or physically abused for being LGBT. And because young people are less likely to have financial resources to support themselves if they are cut off from their families, this can lead to considerable hardship, including homelessness, mental health problems, and substance abuse. In the United States, young LGBT people represent a disproportionate number of homeless youth: between 20 and 40 percent.

Considering these possibilities, people need to consider carefully the repercussions of coming out and take advantage of the support that is available. Teachers and guidance counselors, supportive spiritual leaders, therapists, gay friends, and LGBT hotlines can all be valuable resources for gay people who are taking the first steps toward self-acceptance and living openly.

The Greatest Danger: *Not* Coming Out

Considering the pitfalls and challenges, some may wonder why people choose to come out at all. Why do they put themselves through such difficult and even **traumatic** experiences? One reason is because staying hidden away or "in the closet," as it is sometimes called, can be even more damaging. One study has shown that lesbians who disclose their sexuality to friends and family are more content in their personal lives and less likely to engage in harmful behavior. Conversely, individuals who remain closeted or are forced to keep their sexuality a secret are more at risk for suicide and depression.

According to the American Medical Association, "most of the emotional disturbance experienced by gay men and lesbians around their sexual identity is not based on physiological causes but rather is due more to a sense of **alienation** in an unaccepting environment."

Coming Out for Social Change

There are good reasons for LGBT people to consider coming out, beyond issues of self-respect and personal happiness. It has been said that if every LGBT person came out, prejudice and oppression against them would simply cease to exist. Think about it. Once everyone realized that they already knew and respected an LGBT person, the world would inevitably grow more tolerant. By proudly identifying themselves, LGBT people encourage their families and friends to confront their own prejudices toward a "group" to which their own child, sibling, friend, or even parent belongs. Can you see how an individual act of coming out can have an important social and political effect? Multiplied by thousands, by tens of thousands, by millions, the process could make the world a better place for all LGBT people.

This same idea has led to a movement by some of the more radical LGBT activists to publicly "out" famous people—celebrities, professional athletes, actors, prominent business people, religious leaders, and politicians—who have remained closeted for their own reasons. These activists believe that the world needs more positive LGBT role models, and that many of these closeted celebrities— particularly the politicians and religious leaders—are behaving hypocritically, supporting discrimination and holding back the movement toward full civil rights for LGBT people. While many LGBT celebrities are afraid of coming out because it might damage their careers or tarnish their public images, their doing so can send a powerful message, whether they come forward voluntarily or are "outed." Some of them even become heroes. People like Ellen DeGeneres, Cynthia Nixon, and Jason Collins are vital positive role models, providing other LGBT people with the courage to be themselves and offering their fans an opportunity to rethink some of their stereotypes and prejudices.

Privacy versus Progress

Although coming out may be very important to the progress of the LGBT community, the privacy of those people who choose not to come out is also important, whatever their reasons happen to be. Some people come from families or live in communities where coming out would literally be threatening to their lives. In addition, some people who engage in same-sex sexual behavior, either occasionally or exclusively, would never label themselves as LGBT due to their cultural background or community of origin. For LGBT people who are not out, secrecy is a way of life.

Singer Ricky Martin was repeatedly pushed by interviewers, including Barbara Walters in a televised interview, to admit that he was gay. He denied it until 2010, when he made the decision to come out publicly. "I am very blessed to be who I am," he wrote on his website.

No one is immune to the complex tensions involved in coming out; it's a big step for everyone. But just imagine the pressure on those who must do it on a national or global stage. Singer Ricky Martin was an international superstar when rumors that he might be gay began to appear in the media. He hesitated to come out publicly for fear of how it would affect his career, reputation, and family life. It took years for him to take that step, which he finally did in a moving statement on his website. In it, he wrote about what he referred to as his personal truth, and the influence his children had on inspiring him to finally leave the closet.

"(The truth) fills me with strength and courage," Martin said. "This is just what I need especially now that I am the father of two beautiful boys that are so full of light and who, with their outlook, teach me new things every day. To keep living as I did up until today would be to indirectly diminish the glow that my kids were born with. . . . These years in silence and reflection made me stronger and reminded me that acceptance has to come from within and that this kind of truth gives me the power to conquer emotions I didn't even know existed."

TEXT-DEPENDENT QUESTIONS

- What are the steps involved in the coming-out process?

- What are some of the risks and repercussions that face LGBT people who come out?

- What are some of the benefits to LGBT people who come out?

- What is the right time of life for an LGBT individual to come out?

 RESEARCH PROJECTS

- Make a list of risks that you might face in coming out, and how you would deal with them.

- Read some biographies or biographical essays on people who came out in the 1960s, 1970s, and 1980s. What challenges did they face that still confront LGBT people today?

- Rank the people in your life, from those who would be easiest to come out to, to those who you think would be hardest.

- Many prominent people are "outed" and must then decide how to deal with it. What do you think of this? Write down the pros and cons of outing others, and how you might feel and respond if you were in their situation.

Singer-songwriter Katy Perry rose to stardom in 2008 with her breakthrough single "I Kissed a Girl." The song was in heavy rotation on radio stations and raised awareness of sexual love between women.

2

SARAH'S STORY

 WORDS TO UNDERSTAND

Derogatory: Critical or cruel, as in a term used to make a person feel
devalued or humiliated.
Mentor: Someone who teaches and offers support to another, often
younger, person.
Harassed: Teased, bullied, or physically threatened on an ongoing
basis.

Like most little girls, Sarah Carlin enjoyed playing with her Barbie dolls.
She kept a diary. She spied on older kids in the neighborhood. And she
looked forward to growing up.

She also started to have feelings that she knew made her different.

When she was about nine years old, her family lived across the street
from the small local high school. She would sit on her porch and watch
two girls sneak outside the school and kiss. "For some reason I was so
intrigued," she says. "I wondered why they had to sneak around. I was
so confused because my mom and dad had never told me about two girls
or two boys kissing."

Sarah had already begun to recognize her interest in other girls, though her highest level of experimentation had been having her Barbie dolls kiss each other. But it was enough to make her identify with the girls she saw.

There's nothing that unusual about Sarah's story. Studies show that people—regardless of their sexual orientation—begin to experience sexual attraction between the ages of ten and twelve. As we've noted, LGBTQ youths are recognizing the nature of these feelings and coming out earlier than ever before—due at least in part to the fact that there are more role models for them to identify with, both in the media and the real world.

"It's Just a Phase"

However, LGBTQ gay kids are not necessarily treated exactly the same as straight ones. As Eileen Ross, the director of the Outlet Program, a support service for LGBTQ youth in Mountain View, California, puts it, "When heterosexual boys first indicate their interest in girls, no one says to them, 'Are you sure? You're too young to know if you like girls. It's probably just a phase.' We deny them their feelings and truth in a way we would never do with a heterosexual young person."

The consequences of such a response can be severe. Caitlin Ryan, a researcher at San Francisco State University, spent more than seven years studying the link between how families respond to a gay child coming out and the child's mental health in early adulthood. She found that when teens were rejected by their families, they were more likely to have attempted suicide, used drugs, or suffered depression than were those raised by families who accepted them. The "rejecting behaviors" identified by the study include verbal and physical abuse, the use of **derogatory** terms for gay people, and the forbidding of children to associate with other gay and lesbian youth.

Sarah experienced those behaviors firsthand when her mother saw the same two girls kissing. Sarah admits that she was deeply affected by her mom's reaction.

"She saw the two girls and said, 'Ugh! Girls kissing is not right! That's gross, Sarah!'" she recalls. "I didn't know why, but I felt ashamed and sad. It was like I had to give up something within myself. That is probably when I began to really try my hardest to push any feelings of liking a girl out of my head."

Trying to Be "Normal"

In an effort to fit in with the straight kids at school and make her family proud, Sarah did what many young people do: She tried to be someone else. She had boyfriends in middle school and high school and worked hard at acting like a typical straight girl. But the more she tried to be "normal," the more she felt the negative effects on her life.

"I was so sad because I didn't want this, but I knew it was what I had to do and be," she explains.

Then, in her junior year of high school, Sarah learned that one of her friends was a lesbian, and so was her favorite teacher. Finally, she wasn't alone anymore! There were people who might understand her true nature. There were people just like her.

"She became my **mentor**," Sarah says of her teacher. "I felt like she could know about me and could maybe even help me. She told me that there was a life out there, outside of my class of ninety-seven kids, and that I could be who I was. I felt relieved, but so scared. I made a plan to go to college and then tell my mom and dad over the phone—and then hang up on them. That is not what happened."

A Betrayal of Trust

At the time, Sarah was being treated for depression and an eating disorder, and she had come to rely on and trust her therapist. She needed support, so she overcame her fear and decided to come out to her therapist—a common first step for many LGBTQ people.

"I went in and almost threw up, I was so nervous," she says.

Unable to say the words, she wrote "I think I'm gay" on a piece of paper, folded it over and over again, and finally handed it to her therapist. She waited for a response, unable to make eye contact, terrified at what the reaction would be.

"My therapist opened the piece of paper and shook her head and kind of chuckled," Sarah recalls. "She said, 'Sarah, I've been waiting for you to tell me because I already knew. Your mother called here about two months ago, saying that she had read your journal and thought you were gay.'"

Sarah was furious that her privacy had been violated. She felt betrayed by her own parents. Though she wanted to continue with her plan and remain closeted until she left home for college, she was overcome by emotion and couldn't contain it. When her mother picked her up from the therapist's office, Sarah confronted her with the truth.

"She looked like she had just seen a ghost," Sarah says. "I began crying and so did she."

This kind of dramatic scenario is not uncommon, according to Eileen Ross. *That's not how we raised you. How did this happen? It's not right. It's just a phase. You'll outgrow it.* Though it only lasted for about ten minutes, it was a turning point in Sarah's life.

"I wanted to scream at her, but I couldn't find my voice," Sarah says. "I don't remember much except for being miserable for about a year."

PFLAG (formerly known as Parents, Families, and Friends of Lesbians and Gays) is an organization that helps parents, friends, siblings, and others accept and support LGBT young people.

Seeking Allies—and Acceptance

For the rest of her time in high school, Sarah struggled with finding her way out of the closet on her own. Without the benefit of a gay–straight alliance at her school, she could only confide in a few trusted friends and teachers. She didn't feel ready to come out completely because she didn't know what would happen if she did.

Sexual orientation and gender expression are still some of the most common targets of school bullying, but more and more schools are developing zero-tolerance policies toward bullying or harassment in their halls.

"I went to a small high school and was scared for my safety if I came out," she explains.

She had good reason to be concerned. In a survey conducted by the Gay, Lesbian, and Straight Education Network (GLSEN), 81 percent of LGBT middle school students report being regularly **harassed** at school because of their sexual orientation or gender identity, and 39 percent have been physically assaulted. Even worse, only 29 percent of those who reported bullying to school officials feel that it was handled effectively. When there is no support at school, young people rely even more on their families. In Sarah's case, that wasn't much of an option.

"My dad didn't really speak to me for a while," she says. "He acted like he would 'catch the gayness' if he got too close."

Eventually, her mother sought out more information. She attended PFLAG meetings with Sarah, met Sarah's gay friends, and gradually became more accepting.

"But still, to this day, she doesn't say 'gay,'" Sarah says. "She calls it 'that way.'"

Over time, Sarah's relationship with her parents improved. She went to college, began dating, and lived openly, embracing her sexual identity. She is quick to acknowledge how brave it is for young people to come out in high school—and she has some advice for them.

"Whenever they come out, it has to be when *they* decide," she says. "But no matter what, they need to know that they can be happy and be themselves."

CLOSE-UP: COMING OUT ON THE INTERNET

As studies clearly show, it makes a significant difference for people who are coming out to have support from friends and colleagues. The Internet makes such support easy to find, and offers many forums where newly out LGBT people can share their struggles, problems, and victories with others who are going through the same thing. Here's a post from a Tumblr blog called "When I Came Out..." (whenicameout.tumblr.com):

I just turned 14 yrs old. I have always been in touch with my manly side. My friends always thought I wanted to be a dude, and I guess that is somewhat true. I never really considered myself as gay in any way, but last year I met one of my best friends, Allison, who helped me out a lot. I told her one time I had 3 secrets, and 2 of them I was okay telling her, but the third I was really nervous over. So I sat there texting her until I felt really comfortable and I just came out and said it. And she said she had been able to tell the whole time due to her "gaydar" and that she was also. She said not many people knew, but since I trusted her enough to tell her, she would trust me enough for me to know. Well, I did crush on Allison, it's hard not to when you trust someone that much. I've known I'm half gay for 2 years now. Last night Allison and I were talking and I told her I was tired of hiding who I was, so I sent out a mass text to about 10 of my friends and told them. I told them they should spread it, I wanted them to spread it. There are 2 weeks left of middle school and if I get harassed, whatever. I won't know any of these people besides my friends next year because I will be going to a completely different school. If I get beat up, at least it is because I am myself. So thanks, Allison. I'm looking forward to Tuesday.

TEXT-DEPENDENT QUESTIONS

- What are some of the ways parents and other authority figures discourage early signs of same-sex attraction in kids?
- How do some LGBT people (like Sarah) respond to their parents' rejection of their true selves?
- What are some of the negative consequences of an LGBT youth striving to earn approval by being "normal"?

 RESEARCH PROJECTS

- Write a short narrative about how Sarah's coming-out process might have been different if her school had had a gay–straight alliance.
- Ask some older LGBT people about how they get along with their parents, and the ways those relationships have changed over the years.
- Read (or watch) coming-out stories on the Internet, paying attention to the wide range of problems people have faced and the variety of solutions they've come up with to deal with those challenges.

Gene Robinson became the first openly gay American Episcopal Bishop when he was consecrated in 2003, paving the way for other gay and lesbian religious leaders.

3

ED'S STORY

 WORDS TO UNDERSTAND

Clinical: A medical term referring to the observation and treatment of actual patients (the opposite of *theoretical*).
Repudiation: Dismissal and abandonment.
Isolated: Solitary; cut off from others.

From the time he was a teenager, Ed Wesley knew he was gay. He had his first boyfriend when he was eighteen years old and attempted his first step toward coming out when he was twenty-one.

That's when he confided in his campus minister, who recommended that Ed tell his parents and then go to an ex-gay ministry.

"They treated it like it was an addiction," says Ed. "They told me it was not in God's plan for me."

The reaction was crushing to Ed, a devout Christian who prized his spiritual life above all else. The notion that being gay was a sin or against the will of God forced him back in the closet.

It was nearly fifteen years before he ventured out again. "It was my thirty-fifth birthday," he says, "and I had the realization that I didn't want to live the next thirty-five years like I had the first thirty-five."

Spending Decades in the Closet

Ed's experience is very similar to that of thousands of other LGBT people, whether religious or not. In fact, many wait much longer to embrace their identity. According to Chris Kraft, the **clinical** director at the Johns Hopkins Sexual Behaviors Consultation Unit, men who decide to come out late in adulthood have often known about their sexual orientation since their youth but did not want to risk telling others. One of the biggest reasons for this is the effect it will have on their families and the prospect of being faced with **repudiation** by the people closest to them—which is just what happened to Ed.

"I was always afraid I was going to lose the love of my parents and that I wouldn't be allowed to come home again if they knew I was gay," he says. "They always said I could tell them anything, but the one time I tried, the reaction they had made me close up."

Those fears have kept many people in the closet for their entire lives. But as LGBT rights issues grab headlines in the news and positive LGBT characters are increasingly common in movies and on television, thousands of people have made the decision to come out late in life. The filmmaker Beatrice Alda, along with her wife, Jennifer Brooke, created the documentary *Out Late* to capture the experiences of people who wait until their golden years to embrace their sexual or gender identity.

Explains Alda, "For me, the message is, you have one life, and if you can find a way to get to be who you really are before life ends, that's a gift." She married Brooke in Canada in 2006.

Sometimes people in the LGBT community wait an entire lifetime before they claim their full identities. These two women waited 31 years to be together legally before the state of California allowed them to marry.

Torn Between Faith and Feeling

For years, Ed was told that he couldn't be gay and still have the most important thing in his life—his faith. So he stayed in the closet. Even when he travelled as a consultant in education, he still couldn't be himself. What would his family say? What would happen to his career? He had been honored with a Parent's Choice Award for his performing art. What would the officials think if they knew he was gay?

Those questions haunted him so much that he shut himself off from romantic relationships and didn't explore what it meant to be gay. For more than a decade, denying who he was left a gaping hole in his life where love and romance were meant to be.

While in graduate school, Ed was taking a psychology class when he heard something that stuck with him. "If you're not happy," the professor said, "you need to change something."

Coming Out to God

A short time later, Ed had completed his master's degree—a notable personal success that should have made him proud and happy. Instead, he was thinking about suicide. As he sat in church, surrounded by friendly people he should've considered his community, he felt lonely and **isolated**. When he watched television or listened to music, all he could focus on were the messages about love—heterosexual love. He knew that love was for other people and not for him, so he felt lost, out of place, and angry.

"It didn't make sense to me. Why would God want me to suffer?" he recalls.

As he celebrated his thirty-fifth birthday and reflected on his life so far, he shook his fist at God in fury. Then he got down on his knees and took a step that was very important to him in his coming-out process. It felt much more personal than coming out to his family, his friends, or even his minister.

"I was coming out to God. I was telling God who I was," Ed says. "I thought about the pain of the past. I had spent all that time denying myself the opportunity to love another person because I couldn't love myself. And I couldn't love myself because I thought God didn't love me the way I was."

 CLOSE-UP: COMING OUT TO IMMIGRANT PARENTS

Many countries are more conservative than the United States, and LGBT children of immigrants often find that the prejudices and fears of these faraway cultures add an extra layer of difficulty when coming out. Add to that the fact that many immigrants have high aspirations for their children, which can cause those children to be especially afraid of disappointing them. BuzzFeedYellow's "Coming Out to Immigrant Parents" video features several intriguing stories, including Joel's:

> My parents both grew up in Mexico. My mom is very religious, from a very conservative family. My mom started to cry, and she said, "Well, I know a lot of depressed people that became gay, and I think you're gay because you haven't been going to church the last four years." I was like, "I'm not going to change who I am," and she was like, "You're a bad person." The person that should be giving you unconditional love is telling you you're a bad person. My mom said that. And I broke, I was just like, "Fine. You don't have to have a son who's gay. You don't have to have a son at all. I'm leaving this house. You don't ever have to see me again." My dad was like, "You will not leave this household," and he blocked the door, and then they all came and hugged me, and they were like, "We love you, please stay." And I just started crying. . . . For those of you who are still in the closet, just have hope. It's what kept me going.

Learning from Someone Else's Regrets

Ed then turned to a friend he'd known since his childhood. He took a deep breath, carefully chose his words, and told him what he had been waiting more than a decade to express out loud. What he heard in return surprised him.

"I told him I was gay, and he said he was, too," Ed says. "I was stunned, just stunned."

His friend was older than Ed and married with children. He was active in his church and was living the life he felt was expected of him. He was happy, he said, but had many regrets. And he didn't want to see his good friend take the same path.

"He told me not to make the same mistakes he had," Ed says. "That really had an effect on me. It made me see everything differently."

When Ed recognized the impact that denying his true nature could have on his life, he knew what he had to do. He just wasn't sure how to do it.

That fall, he accepted a position teaching computer classes on a cruise ship. At sea, away from his home and the ties to his past, Ed decided he was going to live his life out loud and proud.

"My friend told me that you have to be comfortable in your own skin before anyone else will accept you," he explains. "That's so true. Working on ships represented the opportunity for me to live openly and not have it matter at all. I could be who I was, and nobody cared."

Accepting Yourself as You Are

That experience helped Ed to accept himself fully, but he still wasn't quite sure what it meant to be gay. He hadn't known many gay people;

Gay urban enclaves, such as San Francisco's Castro district, provide space and support that help many to live openly for the first time in their lives.

everything he knew came from what he'd read or seen on television and in movies. And those gay people didn't quite seem like him.

"Those guys are handsome models with perfect bodies. I'm a big guy," says Ed, who has a husky frame, bald-shaved head, and a goatee. "We don't have gay role models, gay fathers who can mentor us. We don't see ordinary-looking guys who are like us on TV or in movies. That makes it very difficult to find an image of a gay person we can relate to."

While in Los Angeles on a business trip, Ed turned to two of his friends, both openly gay. They offered the support, wisdom, and assistance he had been missing all those years.

"They basically gave me gay culture lessons," he says with a smile. "We went to West Hollywood, the gay area of LA, and I'd never seen anything like it before. There was no judgment. You could be gay, and it didn't matter to anyone."

Ed felt so comfortable in that environment that about a year later he relocated to the Los Angeles area. He put a rainbow sticker on his car, became active in the community, and was finally comfortable in his own skin. It didn't take long for him to begin a relationship, his first in nearly twenty years.

Embracing a New Faith Community

So, how did all of this change affect Ed's faith? That part of his life is still thriving. He has a deep and meaningful relationship with God, which he can express openly. The church he considers home welcomes everyone,

Increasing numbers of Christian churches affirm their welcome to everyone, allowing LGBT individuals to live and worship openly.

and emblazons the words "You're accepted here" all over its publications. Ed enjoys expressing his faith by playing drums in the church band and singing hymns of praise. Finally, he can truly be himself—a devoted Christian, a successful professional, a productive member of the community, and a gay man.

Ed still returns home to Kentucky often in order to visit his parents. He has never formally come out to them since that first time, when he was twenty-one, and his mother continues to quiz him about having kids and getting married.

"I think my parents know, but they've never accepted it," he says. "I'm still Ed Wesley. The fact that I'm a gay man doesn't change anything. And I have to respect their opinion and not force them to accept me."

While the situation may not be perfect, Ed appreciates the fact that other members of his family know he's gay and accept him. And, more importantly, he accepts himself.

"No one ever asked me if I wanted to be gay," he says. "It definitely would have been a lot easier for me if I were straight, in terms of my family, church, business. But I am gay. And I spent many years trying to be somebody I'm not. I think about how different my life would have been [if I'd come out sooner], but that's in the past. This is where I am now, and my life is complete."

TEXT-DEPENDENT QUESTIONS

- What are some of the fears that keep people in the closet for much of their adult life?
- Is it important to formally come out to everyone in your life?
- How important is it in gay male culture to conform to a physical ideal?

 RESEARCH PROJECTS

- Examine the gay male role models in today's culture. See how many you can find who don't conform to current standards of beauty and physical perfection.
- Look up some of the major religions' objections to homosexuality; then find responses and rebuttals to them by LGBT people of faith.
- Talk to an older LGBT person who is active in a church or faith community. Ask about his or her struggles to reconcile sexuality or gender identity with spirituality.

Betty DeGeneres has been active with PFLAG and other LGBT groups since her daughter Ellen came out publicly on her television sitcom *Ellen*.

4

FINDING SUPPORT

 WORDS TO UNDERSTAND

Advocating: Standing up for someone or something.

Discrimination: When someone is treated differently because of his or her race, sexual identity, religion, or some other factor.

Empathy: Feeling for another person; putting yourself mentally and emotionally in another person's place.

Cisgender: Someone who self-identifies with the gender he or she was assigned at birth.

Vitriol: Nastiness; a strong, hostile reaction expressed in speech or writing.

Controversy: A touchy subject about which differing opinions can create tension and strong reactions.

In 1972, Jeanne Manford proudly joined her gay son, Morty, as he marched in New York's Pride Day parade. She was surprised when LGBT people she'd never met came up to her and asked for her assistance in speaking with their own parents. She immediately saw a widespread need for such assistance.

The following spring, Jeanne organized the first meeting of a support group for parents whose children had come out. The session was held at a local church and was attended by about twenty people.

More than thirty-five years later, that small group has become PFLAG—an acronym for Parents, Families (and Friends) of Lesbians and Gays—and has more than 200,000 members who meet in thousands of chapters all over the country. Most parents find their way to those meetings in the spirit that Jeanne had hoped they would: to show their support for their kids and to seek better understanding of the issues they face.

"It's parental. It's an instinctual response to protect their own children," says Ron Schlittler, former PFLAG deputy executive director. "So many parents are not born activists. They don't come by this naturally."

Politicizing Parents

In fact, many parents who never would have considered themselves activists or spokespeople find themselves suddenly taking on that role out of love for their own LGBT children. That was the case for Betty DeGeneres. Her daughter, actress/comedian Ellen DeGeneres, made headlines around the world when she came out publicly on her prime-time sitcom. It didn't take long for her mother, Betty, to become a part of the story, and recognize the significance of her new role.

"The fact that I'm a mom **advocating** equal rights for my daughter and her partner underscores the point that ending discrimination based on sexual orientation is not just important to gay people, it's important to their families and the people who love them," she told *HRC Quarterly*.

At around the same time, she became the first straight spokesperson for National Coming Out Day.

"For too long, gay Americans have suffered **discrimination**," she said in a televised public service announcement that coincided with the annual event. "As long as our sons and daughters are excluded from the basic protection of law, we must share that burden as a family."

A mother holds up a sign as she celebrates, with other members of the Kansas City chapter of PFLAG, the U.S. Supreme Court decision legalizing marriage equality in all 50 states on June 26, 2015.

Gay Acceptance: A Generational Shift

When coming out, LGBT people—especially young ones—tend to turn to their friends for support first. One reason for this is that younger people tend to be more accepting of LGBT people. A Gallup Poll shows that 54 percent of Americans find homosexuality acceptable, but that figure is nearly 10 percent higher among people ages 18-29.

"You're not friends with someone just because they're straight, so why wouldn't you be friends with someone if they're gay?" asks Mollie Sachs. "It's just part of who they are." Mollie is straight and married, but she has numerous colleagues and close friends who are openly gay. Though she has never had a family member come out to her, she **empathizes** with what the experience must be like. But she also knows it would never change the way she feels about someone she loves.

"I can understand why some people might be surprised if they find out their friend or family member is gay," she says. "It can have a big impact on a person's life. But if you accept someone, then you accept everything about them. You can't pick and choose."

Guidelines for New LGBT Allies

When an LGBT person decides to come out, his or her supportive friends and family often want to help make the process easier, but they don't know how. The most important thing that straight people can do for their LGBT friends and family members is to learn more about what it means to be LGBT. One place to turn for this kind of information is a booklet called *Coming Out as a Supporter*, issued by the HRC in partnership with PFLAG.

Maybe you always suspected. Maybe it's a total surprise. But no matter what, when a friend, loved one, or acquaintance makes the decision to come out to you as lesbian, gay, bisexual, or transgender, it is always a significant event. It can spur a range of emotions, from confused to concerned, awkward to honored. It may be hard to know how to react or what you can do to be supportive.

Many people respond initially with confusion, shock, or even anger and fear. The HRC/PFLAG guide recommends asking honest questions that communicate both interest and support. Talking openly and exhibiting a willingness to learn more is a great first step toward living an "LGBT-friendly" life and safeguarding your relationships with LGBT friends and family members.

HRC offers these specific suggestions for demonstrating support:

- Create social settings that bring your straight, **cisgender,** and LGBT friends and family together.

- Talk openly and honestly with your LGBT loved ones about their lives.

- Find opportunities to talk openly with your straight, cis friends about your LGBT friends and family and the issues they face.

- Make sure that you include your LGBT loved one's partner in events and activities, just as you would any other friend's or child's spouse or significant other.

- Don't allow anti-LGBT jokes or statements expressed in your presence to go unchallenged.

The Trauma of "Outing"

The key to offering support to someone who is coming out is respect for his or her feelings and privacy. This includes recognizing when someone hasn't actually made the choice to come out. "Outing"—the revelation by or innuendo by another party that someone is LGBT—takes the power of decision making and control away from the individual. It can leave the person feeling confused, betrayed, and embarrassed.

Actor Neil Patrick Harris encountered just such a situation when his sexual orientation became the source of much speculation in the media. Though he had been living openly in his private life for years, he had decided not to publicly come out. But as rumors spread that he was gay, many people became frustrated that this beloved stage and television actor—and popular awards-show host—chose not to speak out as an advocate for LGBT rights.

"The Internet stuff threw me for a loop because I didn't understand where the **vitriol** was coming from," Harris says. "I thought I had been representing well, and in turn it seemed like I was quickly condemned to step to the plate."

Though frustrated by the pressure, attention, and **controversy**, Harris finally decided to make a public statement about his sexuality:

The public eye has always been kind to me, and until recently I have been able to live a pretty normal life. Now, it seems there is speculation and interest in my private life and relationships. So, rather than ignore those who choose to publish their opinions without actually talking to me, I am happy to dispel any rumors or misconceptions and am quite proud to say that I am a very content gay man living my life to the fullest and feel most fortunate to be working with wonderful people in the business I love.

Regardless of the circumstances, the way friends and family react when someone comes out can have a significant impact on that person's self-esteem and self-confidence. People must decide for themselves how they want to respond. But, to Sarah Carlin, who relied heavily on her close friends when she came out in high school, the matter is simple.

"Stay true to your friends," she says. "They were your friends before you knew they were gay, and it should be no different after."

 TEXT-DEPENDENT QUESTIONS

- What is the relationship between acceptance of LGBT rights and age?
- What are some important pieces of advice you can give someone whose loved one has just come out?
- Do you now feel that outing a closeted LGBT person is a valid means of advancing LGBT acceptance? Why or why not?

 RESEARCH PROJECTS

- Visit the PFLAG website (www.community.pflag.org) and read through the organization's programs, initiatives, and events.
- If you have LGBT friends or relatives with supportive parents, ask those parents about their personal journeys to acceptance.
- Make a list of the ways a person's future might be harmed by being outed before he or she is ready to come out voluntarily.

🔑 SERIES GLOSSARY

Activists: People committed to social change through political and personal action.

Advocacy: The process of supporting the rights of a group of people and speaking out on their behalf.

Alienation: A feeling of separation and distance from other people and from society.

Allies: People who support others in a cause.

Ambiguous: Something unclear or confusing.

Anonymous: Being unknown; having no one know who you are.

Assumption: A conclusion drawn without the benefit of real evidence.

Backlash: An adverse reaction by a large number of people, especially to a social or political development.

Bias: A tendency or preference toward a particular perspective or ideology that interferes with the ability to be impartial, unprejudiced, or objective.

Bigotry: Stubborn and complete intolerance of a religion, appearance, belief, or ethnic background that differs from one's own.

Binary: A system made up of two, and only two, parts.

Bohemian: Used to describe movements, people, or places characterized by nontraditional values and ways of life often coupled with an interest in the arts and political movements.

Caricature: An exaggerated representation of a person.

Celibate: Choosing not to have sex.

Chromosome: A microscopic thread of genes within a cell that carries all the information determining what a person is like, including his or her sex.

Cisgender: Someone who self-identifies with the gender he or she was assigned at birth.

Civil rights: The rights of a citizen to personal and political freedom under the law.

Clichés: Expressions that have become so overused—stereotypes, for example—that they tend to be used without thought.

Closeted: Choosing to conceal one's true sexual orientation or gender identity.

Compensating: Making up for something by trying harder or going further in the opposite direction.

Conservative: Cautious; resistant to change and new ideas.

Controversy: A disagreement, often involving a touchy subject about which differing opinions create tension and strong reactions.

Customs: Ideas and ways of doing things that are commonly understood and shared within a society.

Demonize: Portray something or someone as evil.

Denominations: Large groups of religious congregations united under a common faith and name, and organized under a single legal administration.

Derogatory: Critical or cruel, as in a term used to make a person feel devalued or humiliated.

Deviation: Something abnormal; something that has moved away from the standard.

Dichotomy: Division into two opposite and contradictory groups.

Discrimination: When someone is treated differently because of his or her race, sexual orientation, gender identity, religion, or some other factor.

Disproportionate: A situation where one particular group is overrepresented within a larger group.

Diverse: In the case of a community, one that is made up of people from many different backgrounds.

Effeminate: A word used to refer to men who have so-called feminine qualities.

Emasculated: Having had one's masculinity or manhood taken away.

Empathy: Feeling for another person; putting yourself mentally and emotionally in another person's place.

Empirical evidence: Factual data gathered from direct observation.

Empowering: Providing strength and energy; making someone feel powerful.

Endocrinologist: A medical doctor who specializes in the treatment of hormonal issues.

Epithets: Words or terms used in a derogatory way to put a person down.

The Establishment: The people who hold influence and power in society.

Extremist: Someone who is in favor of using extreme or radical measures, especially in politics and religion.

Flamboyant: Colorful and a bit outrageous.

Fundamentalist: Someone who believes in a particular religion's fundamental principles and follows them rigidly. When the word is used in connection with Christianity, it refers to a member of a form of Protestant Christianity that believes in the strict and literal interpretation of the Bible.

Gay liberation: The movement for the civil and legal rights of gay people that originated in the 1950s and emerged as a potent force for social and political change in the late 1960s and '70s.

Gender: A constructed sexual identity, whether masculine, feminine, or entirely different.

Gender identity: A person's self-image as female, male, or something entirely different, no matter what gender a person was assigned at birth.

Gender roles: Those activities and traits that are considered appropriate to males and females within a given culture.

Gene: A microscopic sequence of DNA located within a chromosome that determines a particular biological characteristic, such as eye color.

Genitalia: The scientific term for the male and female sex organs.

Genocide: The large-scale murder and destruction of a particular group of people.

Grassroots: At a local level; usually used in reference to political action that begins within a community rather than on a national or global scale.

Harassed/harassment: Being teased, bullied, or physically threatened.

Hate crime: An illegal act in which the victim is targeted because of his or her race, religion, sexual orientation, or gender identity.

Homoerotic: Having to do with homosexual, or same-sex, love and desire.

Homophobia: The fear and hatred of homosexuality. A homophobic person is sometimes referred to as a "homophobe."

Horizontal hostility: Negative feeling among people within the same minority group.

Hormones: Chemicals produced by the body that regulate biological functions, including male and female gender traits, such as beard growth and breast development.

Identity: The way a person, or a group of people, defines and understands who they are.

Inborn: Traits, whether visible or not, that are a part of who we are at birth.

Inclusive: Open to all ideas and points of view.

Inhibitions: Feelings of guilt and shame that keep us from doing things we might otherwise want to do.

Internalized: Taken in; for example, when a person believes the negative opinions other people have of him, he has *internalized* their point of view and made it his own.

Interpretation: A particular way of understanding something.

Intervention: An organized effort to help people by changing their attitudes or behavior.

Karma: The force, recognized by both Hindus and Buddhists, that emanates from one's actions in this life; the concept that the good and bad things one does determine where he or she will end up in the next life.

Legitimized: Being taken seriously and having the support of large numbers of people.

LGBT: An initialism that stands for lesbian, gay, bisexual, and transgender. Sometimes a "Q" is added (**LGBTQ**) to include "questioning." "Q" may also stand for "queer."

Liberal: Open to new ideas; progressive; accepting and supportive of the ideas or identity of others.

Liberation: The act of being set free from oppression and persecution.

Mainstream: Accepted, understood, and supported by the majority of people.

Malpractice: When a doctor or other professional gives bad advice or treatment, either out of ignorance or deliberately.

Marginalize: Push someone to the sidelines, away from the rest of the world.

Mentor: Someone who teaches and offers support to another, often younger, person.

Monogamous: Having only one sexual or romantic partner.

Oppress: Keep another person or group of people in an inferior position.

Ostracized: Excluded from the rest of a group.

Out: For an LGBT person, the state of being open with other people about his or her sexual orientation or gender identity.

Outed: Revealed or exposed as LGBT against one's will.

Persona: A character or personality chosen by a person to change the way others perceive them.

Pioneers: People who are the first to try new things and experiment with new ways of life.

Politicized: Aware of one's rights and willing to demand them through political action.

Prejudice: An opinion (usually unfavorable) of a person or a group of people not based on actual knowledge.

Proactive: Taking action taken in advance of an anticipated situation or difficulty.

Progressive: Supporting human freedom and progress.

Psychologists and psychiatrists: Professionals who study the human mind and human behavior. Psychiatrists are medical doctors who can prescribe pills, whereas clinical psychologists provide talk therapy.

Quackery: When an untrained person gives medical advice or treatment, pretending to be a doctor or other medical expert.

The Right: In politics and religion, the side that is generally against social change and new ideas; often used interchangeably with *conservative*.

Segregation: Historically, a system of laws and customs that limited African Americans' access to many businesses, public spaces, schools, and neighborhoods that were "white only."

Sexual orientation: A person's physical and emotional attraction to the opposite sex (heterosexuality), the same sex (homosexuality), both sexes (bisexuality), or neither (asexuality).

Sociologists: People who study the way groups of humans behave.

Spectrum: A wide range of variations.

Stereotype: A caricature; a way to judge someone, probably unfairly, based on opinions you may have about a particular group they belong to.

Stigma: A mark of shame.

Subculture: A smaller group of people with similar interests and lifestyles within a larger group.

Taboo: Something that is forbidden.

Theories: Ideas or explanations based on research, experimentation, and evidence.

Tolerance: Acceptance of, and respect for, other people's differences.

Transgender: People who identify with a gender different from the one they were assigned at birth.

Transphobia: Fear or hatred of transgender people.

Variance: A range of differences within a category such as gender.

Victimized: Subjected to unfair and negative treatment, including violence, bullying, harassment, or prejudice.

FURTHER RESOURCES

PFLAG National
(formerly, Parents, Families, and Friends of Lesbians and Gays).
www.community.pflag.org

Coming Out Center
The Human Rights Campaign's page for coming-out news, support, and resources.
www.hrc.org/campaigns/coming-out-center

How to Come Out as a Gay or Lesbian Teen
A 10-step guide for young people from Wiki How.
www.wikihow.com/Come-Out-As-a-Gay-or-Lesbian-Teen

When I Came Out
An open community board featuring coming-out stories from around the world.
whenicameout.com

Coming Out as a Supporter
A guide for straight people who want to be effective allies the fight for LGBT equality.
www.hrc.org/resources/entry/straight-guide-to-lgbt-americans

GLBT National Help Center
A national hotline for people with questions about sexual orientation and gender identity.
www.glbthotline.org

The Trevor Project
Crisis intervention and suicide prevention services for LGBTQ people ages 13–24.
www.thetrevorproject.org

Coming Out Support
Frequently asked questions, advice, and more from Britain's LGBT Foundation.
www.lgbt.foundation/information-advice/coming-out-support

INDEX